ARCHITECTURE & DESIGN LIBRARY

TOWN HOUSES

TOWN HOUSES

Ann Rooney Heuer

FRIEDMAN/FAIRFAX
PUBLISHERS

A FRIEDMAN/FAIRFAX BOOK

Friedman/Fairfax Publishers
15 West 26 Street
New York, NY 10010
Telephone (212) 685-6610
Fax (212) 685-1307
Please visit our website: www.metrobooks.com

Library of Congress Cataloging-in-Publication Data

Heuer, Ann Rooney.
    Townhouses / Ann Rooney Heuer.
        p. cm. -- (Architecture and design library)
    ISBN 1-58663-026-1 (alk. paper)
        1. Row houses. 2. Interior decoration. 3. House furnishings. I. Title. II. Series.

NA7520 .H48 2000
728f.312--dc21

00-037201

Editor: Betsy Beier and Susan Lauzau
Art Director: Jeff Batzli
Designer: John B. Marius
Photography Editor: Erin Feller
Production Manager: Camille Lee

Color separations by Colourscan Overseas Co Pte Ltd.
Printed in Hong Kong by Midas Printing Limited

1 3 5 7 9 10 8 6 4 2

Distributed by Sterling Publishing Company, Inc.
387 Park Avenue South
New York, NY 10016
Distributed in Canada by Sterling Publishing
Canadian Manda Group
One Atlantic Avenue, Suite 105
Toronto, Ontario, Canada M6K 3E7
Distributed in Australia by
Capricorn Link (Australia) Pty Ltd.
P.O. Box 6651
Baulkham Hills, Business Centre, NSW 2153, Australia

For my loving family circle and for Hallie Einhorn and Wendy Missan, two of the talented editors at the Michael Friedman Publishing Group, whose creative touch added beauty and elegance to this town house tribute.

Contents

INTRODUCTION

"The two story [row] houses that were put up in my boyhood forty years ago all had a kind of unity, and many of them were far from unbeautiful."

—H. L. MENCKEN,

BALTIMORE EVENING SUN, FEB. 7, 1927

The centuries-old story of the town house is one of architectural tradition and innovation, modest and grand interiors, and devastating loss and triumphant preservation. Dating back to the Middle Ages, the town house is an architectural classic also known as a "row house," "terrace," and "brownstone," among other names. Town houses are typically two, three, or more stories high, and usually exist as part of a planned complex of tightly sited dwellings. While many town houses are attached, sharing common walls and similar or identical facades with four or more distinct houses in a city block, others are detached, standing slightly apart from their neighbors.

Since the twelfth century, nearly every European city has created its own unique style of town house, such as the arcaded, Romanesque stone town houses of Cluny, France, and the decorative timber-framed medieval "rows" of Chester, England. During the Middle Ages, because land within each city's defensive walls was finite, the stone, brick, and timber homes were narrow in design, featuring two stories and a basement level. Often, the first floor served as a merchant's shop or artisan's work area, while the second floor was a large hall reserved for cooking, eating, entertaining, and sleeping.

During the Renaissance, the minor town houses or "palaces" of Florence, Italy, were often only two or three windows wide, yet their grandeur came from lavish interior courtyards, four stories of living space, and stunning ornamental facades. By the late seventeenth century, the attached English terrace featured three to five floors with separate dining and drawing rooms, bedrooms, and servants' quarters. In France, the more elaborate town house or "hôtel" of wealthy bourgeois families was generally freestanding, offering sumptuous courtyards, gardens, and elegant accommodations.

Across Europe today, from London to Brussels, and from Dublin to Amsterdam, an impressive array of restored antique town houses still exists. Sadly though, a number of treasured European town houses

OPPOSITE: *It has been said that architecture is scenery, and San Francisco's most famous—and most photographed—row of ornate Queen Anne-style town houses illustrates the point. These Painted Ladies, with their elaborate spindlework details, ornamental pediments, classical columns, and varied but harmonious colors, create a striking contrast with the distant skyscrapers of downtown San Francisco.*

were destroyed during World War II, including the distinctive overhanging medieval timber-frame houses in Lisieux, France. More recently, thousands of European town houses have been condemned and demolished because of deteriorating facades, lack of plumbing, or other structural problems. Fortunately, however, in North America and Europe, a newfound appreciation for historically significant buildings, homes, and sites emerged after World War II, supported by such organizations as the National Trust for Historic Preservation, the National Historic Sites and Monuments Board of Canada, and SAVE Britain's Heritage.

Throughout North America today, vintage town houses are considered an architectural legacy that adds stately beauty and a human scale to modern cities. In New York, clusters of preserved town houses and brownstones lend character to countless neighborhoods in Manhattan, Brooklyn, and the Bronx. Symbolic of New York, brownstones are dignified Victorian-era town houses featuring dark, red-brown sandstone facades. Curiously, the term brownstone also refers to any nineteenth-century brick or stone town house. In New York's Greenwich Village, a designated historic district, charming town houses abound, including the city's narrowest row house—a nine-foot (2.7m)-wide dwelling on Bedford Street where poet Edna St. Vincent Millay and actor John Barrymore are said to have resided. Unfortunately, throughout the twentieth century in New York and other North American metropolitan areas, thousands of aging town houses were demolished to make room for high-rise apartment buildings, hotels, department stores, and other modern structures. Thanks to the vision of preservationists and passionate residents, however, countless elegant town houses have been, and continue to be, restored in New York City and beyond.

In Philadelphia for example, the red brick row house, the most common type of home constructed there in the eighteenth and nineteenth centuries, is today esteemed as an architectural treasure. While some historic row houses in the city's commercial district lost their architectural identities when pressed into service as corner grocery stores or bars in the early twentieth century, after World War II, aggressive architectural renovation efforts at the city, state, and federal level have restored the colonial splendor of Philadelphia's hallmark Georgian row houses.

The famed Victorian Painted Ladies of San Francisco have also been lovingly preserved. Their lavish facades grace the city's hilly streetscapes with color and charm. Some of San Francisco's row houses, such as those on Webster Street, have been declared historic landmarks. In Toronto, the restoration of Victorian-era row houses has helped transform the city's Cabbagetown district. Once a quaint nineteenth-century neighborhood where Irish immigrants grew cabbages in their front yards, by 1960 much of Cabbagetown was run-down. The turning point came a few years later when an architect and several enthusiastic college graduates successfully rehabilitated a number of area row houses bought at "fire-sale" prices. As a result, restored town houses with lovely gardens once again ornament Cabbagetown and other historic neighborhoods throughout Canada.

Today, as the cost of desirable real estate rises in cities and suburbs across North America, architects and urban planners continue to capitalize on the town house's space-saving, vertically oriented struc-

OPPOSITE: *It was common for town houses of the early and mid-nineteenth century to repeat such widely accepted facade styles as Federal and Greek Revival. By the 1880s, however, architectural eclecticism called for each town house to vary in appearance from its neighbors. Despite differences in size, window and door design, and more, these two historic brick town houses in Washington, D.C., share a harmonious Italianate spirit, evidenced in such details as bracketed cornices and windows with segmented- or full-arch crowns.*

ture and the synergy of its harmonious facades. For example, during the 1990s, a prime San Francisco city lot measuring only two hundred feet (61m) deep by ninety-five feet (29m) wide became the home to twenty contemporary, shingle-clad, three-story town houses and two apartments. Developed by the firm Urban Frontier, each town house offers a ground-level garage, first-floor lobby and back room, second-floor master suite, and a spacious third-floor great room. In the planned community of Reston, Virginia, established in the 1960s by the Mobil Corporation, a colorful group of town houses shares gorgeous lakefront and woodland acreage with gracious single homes and high-

rise apartment complexes. The town houses' facades vary in style from "Neo-Victorian" sherbet-hued confections, to modern wooden designs with diamond-shaped windows, to charming colonial-style row houses with quaint dormers and shuttered windows. And, in the winter sports mecca of Lake Placid, New York, a number of Adirondack camp-style town houses sided with rough cut boards, birch bark, or cedar shingles were recently built for The Whiteface Club, a luxurious planned mountain community.

Whether you live in a contemporary or traditional town house or you simply want to learn more about town house design and decor, this

lavish guide will open countless doors for you. Throughout the following chapters, you'll visit town houses with abundant curb appeal, thanks to careful attention to exterior details. You'll see how narrow interiors can be remodeled to enhance a sense of space, light, and serenity. From traditional, Federal-style living rooms and elegant Victorian libraries to airy minimalist kitchens and country-style bedrooms and baths, you'll discover a variety of formal and relaxed designs that can enhance the personality of your town house's interior. Throughout the book, you'll also explore secret garden rooms hidden away on town house terraces, balconies, and roof tops, where nature and comfortable garden furnishings conspire to create peaceful "country in the city" havens perfect for relaxation or entertaining.

OPPOSITE: *This charming "home away from home" is actually a rooftop addition to a Chicago, Illinois, town house. Here, several stories above the city streets, a feeling of serenity reigns, for this sanctuary offers an inviting patio embraced by a rustic picket fence, colorful country blooms, and the comfort of blue skies.*

LEFT: *A peek inside the rooftop cottage reveals a simple yet luxurious American country–style bedroom graced with warm wooden floors, rustic beams, and a colorful handmade quilt and rug. Abundant sunlight and fresh flowers bring the outdoors in, while the fireplace offers a cozy retreat for cold winter nights.*

CHAPTER ONE
ARCHITECTURAL STYLES

"Architecture is frozen music."
—MADAME DE STAEL-HOLSTEIN

From the vantage point of the street, a row of restored town houses is a stunning orchestration of brick and stone, wood and glass, and such period accessories as decorative iron railings and lanterns. The repetitious design of each facade, from front door and window placement to the shape and color of the rooftops, creates a delightful rhythm. Still, there is more than aesthetic harmony to be found in a city block lined with lovely old town houses. There is a tangible sense of the past.

You can feel it on Beacon Hill in Boston, where dignified plum-colored brick town houses with curvilinear front bays and recessed, arched doorways recall the popular Federal style of the early nineteenth century. You can experience the antebellum glory days of Savannah when admiring its restored Federal-period, red brick town houses with broad front doors flanked by classical columns. And the Victorian passion for myriad architectural styles, colors, and facade ornamentation can be appreciated in San Francisco, where Painted Lady row houses preserve the rich legacy of the city's post–Gold Rush days.

While modern town house facades often feature streamlined walls of masonry, wood, and glass, restored town houses dating from the Victorian era (1837–1901) often display a wealth of exterior details originally designed to reflect social standing. Understanding the key facade components of the major architectural styles of the nineteenth century

OPPOSITE: *During the 1880s, the tradition of building rows of flat town house facades with uniform cornice lines lost popularity with the emergence of the Queen Anne style. This new style promoted lively ornamental detail and asymmetrical facades and rooflines, as can be seen in this vintage town house. Some common Queen Anne features include bay windows, recessed front or sleeping porches, ornamental garlands, and decorative panels and sunburst forms. Exteriors are usually brick, brownstone, or wood, with large A-form gables and small dormer windows. Turrets and towers, with all their fairy-tale charm, add to the romance of this classic architectural style.*

ABOVE: *Between 1880 and 1900, more than 1,500 people built or remodeled homes in San Francisco. Interestingly, some of the renowned architects of the time added signature details such as custom millwork or cameo face ornaments above the entryway. This lovely San Francisco Painted Lady town house showcases an array of exquisite architectural finery, from the decorative bay window to the sheltered portico and colorful front door.*

can add to the appreciation of the ever-changing, yet timeless, fashions of North American town house design.

Derived from an Anglo-Dutch interpretation of Baroque and Italian Renaissance architecture, the Georgian style (1700–1830) was the most prominent architectural expression in North America until about 1780. Georgian town houses abound in such cities as Toronto, Philadelphia, Boston, and Alexandria, Virginia. Stately Georgian brick or stone facades feature paneled front doors with decorative crowns supported by pilasters, windows with double-hung sashes, and cornices with tooth-like dentils or other decorative moldings.

Federal-style or "Adamesque" (1780–1840) town houses were influenced by the graceful neoclassical designs of England's Adam brothers. Many Federal-style town houses in Washington, D.C.'s historic Georgetown district feature elegant brick facades with neoclassical door surrounds and front doors crowned by fanlights. Other common attributes of the style include iron stair rails and balconies, curved front bays, roofline balustrades, and keystone lintels above windows.

Gracious full-facade and entry porches supported by classical columns are often features of Greek Revival–style (1825–1860) town houses found in such port cities as New Orleans; Richmond, Virginia; and Galveston, Texas. Other common details of the Greek Revival style include a wide band of trim below the cornice of the main and porch roofs, and elaborate door surrounds with front doors embellished by narrow sidelights and transom lights.

Although usually reserved for rural settings, Gothic Revival–style (1840–1880) facades are found on a number of urban town houses in New York. A few attributes of this picturesque medieval style include arched door surrounds, elaborate paneled or rustic batten doors, pointed-arch windows, parapets and castellated towers, polychrome masonry patterns created by contrasting bands of brickwork or stonework, and scroll-sawn trim and window tracery.

The ornate Italianate style (1840–1885) originated in England and promoted villa-like housing designs inspired by Italy's northern farmhouses. From New York City to San Francisco, the Italianate style was the most popular town house design from the 1850s through the 1880s. Key exterior components include brownstone, brick, or painted wooden facades; wide projecting cornices and brackets; tall arched windows; corner quoins; and ornamental door surrounds and window crowns. The Second Empire style (1855–1885) joined the similar Italianate style in dominating urban housing design in North America for several decades. Hallmarks of this style are graceful mansard roofs with dormer windows; decorative molded cornices and brackets; arched windows; and paired entry doors.

The most prominent examples of Stick–style (1860–1890) town house architecture can be seen in San Francisco. A number of San Francisco's Painted Ladies incorporate the style's symphony of details, from the patterned vertical wooden strips or "sticks," to decorative brackets. The showy Queen Anne style (1880–1910) is found on both detached town houses and attached row houses. Detached town houses usually have prominent front-gabled roofs, while flat or side-gabled roofs are seen on row houses. Queen Anne facades generally feature one of four types of decorative detailing: a spindlework motif with gingerbread ornamentation in porch balustrades, friezes, and more; a classical theme expressed through columns, Palladian windows, and cornice line dentils; medieval half-timbering displayed in gables or upper-story walls; or solid patterned masonry with elegant brickwork or stonework accents. Common facade features include porches, bay windows, wall texture variations, gables, and towers.

The Richardson Romanesque style (1880–1900) was commonly seen on detached town houses, but not on row houses. Hallmarks of this popular Victorian town house style include rough-hewn stone facing, front-gabled or mansard roofs, towers, and Romanesque arches around doors and deep-set windows.

During the Gilded Age, a wide variety of architectural styles emerged in what has come to be called the Eclectic movement (1880–1940). Though less common than the styles mentioned above, these varied styles can be found gracing the facades of many town houses throughout North America. The styles include: Colonial Revival (1880–1955); Chateauesque (1880–1910); Beaux Arts (1885–1930); Mission (1890–1920); and Italian Renaissance (1890–1935).

BELOW: *A "brownstone revival" occurred in New York in the 1960s when many city dwellers moved out of apartments and into vintage brownstones in order to escape rising rents. As a result, many deteriorating town houses across the city were renovated and entire neighborhoods of architecturally significant homes were restored. These inviting brick town houses in Greenwich Village have been lovingly restored, to showcase their original nineteenth-century details.*

OPPOSITE: *Many of today's town houses are built in historic neighborhoods and often emulate the character of the surrounding homes through the use of similar building materials, colors, and designs. These attached twentieth-century town houses in Chicago, Illinois, pay homage to the Richardsonian Romanesque style of the late nineteenth century with their bay windows and ground-level rough-faced stonework.*

RIGHT: *Perfectly preserved, these elegant nineteenth-century row houses are found on Jackson Place in Washington, D.C. From the nation's capital to Charleston, South Carolina, it's not uncommon to see southern brick row houses painted pristine white or a decorative pastel hue. Interestingly, up North in Philadelphia, brick town houses are often painted over in their original color—a rich reddish brown. Paint can dramatically alter the impression of a town house's facade, accentuating architectural details and suggesting the illusion of larger or smaller proportions.*

LEFT: *The Queen Anne architectural style became popular after the 1876 Centennial Exposition in Philadelphia, where two British Queen Anne–style buildings with profuse decorative details were displayed. The event was widely publicized and Americans fell in love with the highly ornamental style. This lovely town house celebrates many hallmark features of Queen Anne design, including decorative facade panels and the varied wall texture treatment achieved with patterned shingles.*

RIGHT: *Classic architecture, like a great symphony or opera, has the power to enchant and endure. In cities around the world, soaring Gothic cathedrals and contemporary skyscrapers captivate us with their exquisitely orchestrated designs. On a more intimate scale, the Painted Lady town house, with its profusion of detail and its vibrant coloring, has become an endearing architectural icon in its own right. This decorative Victorian-era Painted Lady harks back to the late nineteenth century, when the passion for facade embellishment produced homes that wore three to five harmonious shades of paint.*

LEFT: *Elegant and sleek, this contemporary cream-colored stone town house offers stunning window views of city life. Its dramatic modern design holds its own against the larger neighboring buildings.*

OPPOSITE: *A rear view of the contemporary cream town house reveals a tranquil terrace. An abundance of lush container gardens and a streamlined metal table and chairs set the scene for a relaxed lunch or dinner party, while the balconies are ideally situated for sunbathing or wishing upon a star.*

ABOVE: *Although narrow in size, this contemporary town house presents a spacious-looking facade and interior. The home's airy ambience is created by its generous expanse of windows, artful lighting, and the ivory color scheme carried through each floor. The stark minimalist decor combines warm wood with strong metal architectural accents, and is punctuated by furnishings in complementary orange and blue.*

RIGHT: *It's said that Italianate houses were more commonly found in San Francisco than any other North American city from 1850 to 1885 because this architectural style was suited for the city's "high building density." The peak of the Italianate style in America also happened to coincide with San Francisco's rise from small town to important port city, and many of the city's earliest town houses were built in this style. Signature Italianate features of these periwinkle blue town houses include tall cornices with decorative brackets, elaborate door and window treatments, and ornate entry porches. While many of San Francisco's early Italianate town houses had flat fronts, later designs often showcased large bay windows.*

RIGHT: *This dramatic juxtaposition of a vintage and modern town house in Amsterdam illustrates the creative possibilities of this enduring architectural style. Perfectly suited for compact city streets, many lovely gabled brick town houses were built along Amsterdam's four main canals from the sixteenth century onward. Today, a number of modern town houses coexist with the ornate homes of yesteryear, displaying sleek, contemporary designs of glass and steel, and vibrant colors and shapes.*

OPPOSITE: *This elegant urban town house in Brooklyn was inspired by the formal facades of nineteenth-century Italianate and Second Empire–style town houses, which often featured triple windows, distinctive corner quoins, and one- or two-story bay windows, among other architectural attributes.*

CHAPTER TWO

MEMORABLE FACADES AND SECRET GARDENS

"The facade of a building does not belong only to those who own it, but all who behold it."

—ANONYMOUS CHINESE POET

In historic neighborhoods such as the Society Hill District of Philadelphia, where many of the landmark town houses share similar Georgian- or Federal-style brick facades, the overall effect is one of balance and harmony. Not surprisingly, houses and buildings listed on the Philadelphia Register of Historic Places are protected from demolition, and their facades cannot be altered without official permission from the Philadelphia Historical Commission. Most of these homes have been lovingly restored in a way that preserves their historical, architectural, and cultural significance. Today, the National Trust for Historic Preservation and numerous statewide and metropolitan historic preservation organizations are able to provide valuable restoration guidelines to owners of designated historic town houses.

For town house owners whose homes are not part of a historic district or a planned community where facade design is regulated, a variety of exterior features can be added that lend subtle individuality while maintaining the architectural esprit de corps of the home and its neighbors. For example, much of a town home's curb appeal lies in the welcoming personality of its front door. Myriad front door styles are available today, from ornate six-paneled neoclassical reproductions to elegant Victorian-style double doors to sleek contemporary steel doors with narrow windows. In Dublin's Fitzwilliam Square, the front doors of antique Georgian "terraces" are often painted a vibrant gold, red, or green to set each town house apart from its neighbors. Without doubt, ornamental or colorful front doors add aesthetic appeal and offer the chance to express individuality without radically changing your home's facade. Painted shutters and trim can also serve as stylish accents to brick, stone, or wooden facades. Some historic town houses in Baltimore, Charleston, and Georgetown have painted pastel-colored brick exteriors and dark shutters that set them off from surrounding homes. The Painted Ladies of San Francisco, with their exuberantly colored facades, provide another vivid example of the power of color in expressing individuality.

OPPOSITE: *Pastel-hued paint and elaborate architectural details enliven the facades of many vintage town houses. This ornate Victorian duplex displays a palette of five paint colors, designed to highlight the decorative moldings.*

Other embellishments that can imbue town house exteriors with character include lush floral wreaths and swags; period light fixtures, door knockers and doorknobs, and mailboxes; and stair railings and fences that maintain the architectural character of the town house. Overflowing window boxes and terra-cotta planters or stone urns parading up wide stoops or stairways or embroidering airy balconies are other stylish touches that will give your town house a decorative boost.

While the flower-bedecked facades of town houses old and new are designed to convey a sense of public welcome, the secret gardens found on backyard town house terraces, balconies, and rooftops have another agenda: privacy, sanctuary, and peace. Part of the joy of creating a town house garden room lies in the fact that it will become an extended living room for family and an idyllic setting for al fresco entertaining.

Casual terraces may feature random flagstones or wooden decking, while more formal terraces often utilize brick or limestone. A romantic rose- or vine-covered pergola or a state-of-the-art retractable awning can add a bit of shade to a sunny terrace, while rooftop gardens benefit from the shelter of patio umbrellas, lattice screens, and clusters of small potted trees.

Furnishing the garden room is easy, as there is an array of traditional and contemporary outdoor furniture available. For the formal town house, wrought-iron look-alikes made of curvaceous steel or cast aluminum are ideal, as are solid teak or synthetic wicker pieces. Other tasteful furnishing styles for formal spaces include English Garden, Mission, and Art Nouveau. For more casual town houses, wooden Adirondack chairs and settees, aluminum chairs with mesh seats, and molded resin furnishings add a carefree summer ambience. The most successful furniture arrangements offer islands of seating designed specifically for conversation, dining, or private reflection.

Make certain that pillows and cushions for outdoor use are crafted from weather-resistant vinyl, acrylic, or polyester fabric, all available in a variety of colors and patterns. Wind chimes, temple chimes, tabletop water fountains, and colorful candles are also popular garden room accessories. Of course, a profusion of hanging baskets and container gardens, from terra-cotta pots to antique urns, are always welcome.

Rooftop container gardens needn't be placed against walls or railings. Some city gardeners have covered their town house rooftops with gravel or stone topped with clusters of colorful containers of flowers that wind across the space, creating garden paths accented with potted shrubs, vines, and cozy garden benches. When choosing the flowers and plants for your rooftop or terrace container gardens, it's wise to select hardy species that will thrive in your region's climate and stand up to the soot or pollution sometimes found in urban environments.

OPPOSITE: *Festooned for the holidays with lavish evergreen wreaths, the facade of this vintage town house hints at the hospitality to be found inside. Classic Adamesque details such as the columned portico, the cornice emphasized with toothlike dentils, the decorative balustrades, and the radiant front door surrounded with fanlights embellish this beautifully preserved facade.*

LEFT: *Each June, this venerable Beacon Hill town house in Boston is the pride of the neighborhood when its clusters of showy purple wisteria blossoms unfold.*

OPPOSITE: *This historic Baltimore town house enchants with its well tended private garden, curved walkway, and pristine red brick facade graced with shuttered windows, a common feature of Georgian, Federal, and Greek Revival style town houses.*

LEFT: *Vibrant, multicolored double doors—a gregarious feature that signals hospitality—open wide to welcome guests into the home. The exuberant red, yellow, and lavender door scheme complements the house's restful green brick exterior.*

RIGHT: *The front gardens of these nineteenth-century brick town houses are at their most spectacular in the springtime, thanks to a profusion of tulips, daffodils, and flowering crabapple and dogwood trees.*

BELOW: *Sometimes one extraordinary architectural feature, such as this town house's neoclassical shell-shaped pediment, is enough to create an unforgettable facade. The dramatic wrought-iron light fixtures and fence, as well as the stately urns and six-paneled door, also lend a classic ambience to the entryway.*

ABOVE: *A riot of hot pink blossoms adds color and curb appeal to the balconies of this sunny San Francisco Italianate-style town house. Such natural jewels can imbue a sedate facade with a delicious sense of romance.*

RIGHT: *It's been estimated that 80 percent of all real estate transactions are inspired by a buyer's first impression. The curbside appeal of this Greenwich Village town house in New York City is undeniable; what first strikes the viewer are the elaborate door surround and sidelights—prominent features of nineteenth-century Federal- and Greek Revival–style town houses. These features, combined with the blue door and the entryway's lush greenery, invest the facade with an air of antiquity and romance.*

ABOVE: *These elegant town houses reflect the surrounding countryside with facades painted in subtle shades of sand, pale blue-gray, terra-cotta, sage, and silver. Note the way white balcony railings complement each town house's white window trim.*

OPPOSITE: *During the nineteenth century, the American poet Walt Whitman observed the "pull-down and build over again spirit" of his country. This spirit prevailed throughout much of the twentieth century, leading to the destruction of large numbers of deteriorating town houses in cities throughout North America. Fortunately, however, numerous conservancy groups and passionate individuals have saved and restored many of these architectural treasures, such as this row of brick-fronted Beacon Hill town houses in Boston.*

ABOVE: *In the county of Cambridgeshire, England, this streetscape of Georgian terrace houses illustrates how a single defining detail can set a home apart from its neighbors. Vividly painted front doors in regal blue, lively red, and striking black boldly define each entryway, displaying touches of individuality in the otherwise uniform row.*

RIGHT: *This romantic street of vintage town houses in the Commonwealth Back Bay area of Boston is a picture of Victorian perfection, from the elaborate architectural styling of each home to the lush, well-tended gardens. The town houses feature spacious sunken basements that, during the nineteenth century, housed kitchens and servants' quarters.*

ABOVE: *This town house rooftop garden room makes a charming spot for a plein air breakfast or lunch, as well as offering stunning views of the Boston skyline. Such rooftop spaces can provide room for "country in the city" gardens filled with potted fruit trees, berry bushes, assorted annuals, herbs, and vegetables. A pergola for growing vines or climbing roses doubles as a shelter for comfortable outdoor furnishings, creating a tranquil, lush setting for private dining or entertaining.*

ABOVE: *Fifteenth-century scholar Desiderius Erasmus described gardens as places that are capable of "rejoicing the eye, refreshing the nose, and renewing the spirit." This terrace garden succeeds in creating an ambience of paradise, thanks to its keen attention to detail, from the stained glass French doors to the inviting Gilded Age table setting surrounded by a profusion of romantic wisteria and frilly petunias.*

ABOVE: *The tradition of rooftop gardening dates back to ancient times, when fruit trees, shrubs, and plants thrived on Roman "towers." This town house rooftop terrace in Bruges, Belgium, is filled with a variety of ornamental foliage plants punctuated by bright shots of pink and purple blooms, continuing the long history of gardens above the ground.*

ABOVE: *Serving tea for two is a pleasure on this cozy town house terrace replete with container gardens and colorful flea market furnishings. The white walls and friendly blooms make the most of the compact space and create a welcome garden room retreat.*

CHAPTER THREE

MAXIMIZING SPACE AND LIGHT

"We shape our buildings; thereafter they shape us."

—SIR WINSTON CHURCHILL

While vintage town houses may soar six stories high and offer breathtaking "treehouse" views of city streets and landmarks, their tall but narrow structure often poses interior design challenges. Many nineteenth- and early twentieth-century town houses feature tunnel-like rooms only thirteen feet (4m) wide, while others stretch to widths of twenty-five feet (7.5m) or more. Typical Victorian-era town houses, though, are narrow and feature several floors filled with a wealth of tiny rooms, from first-floor parlors, libraries, and dining rooms to third-floor bedrooms and dressing rooms. Many of these rooms were compactly constructed to retain the warmth generated by fireplaces. Today, however, central heating makes town house living spaces of all sizes possible.

In recent decades, architects, contractors, and interior designers across North America have updated thousands of vintage town houses to create residences with a sense of spaciousness, light, and elegance suitable for contemporary living. Their creative ideas for maximizing town house dimensions and style involve rethinking the location and function of each room, and accentuating such assets as breathtaking city or garden views or a room's well-preserved architectural accents.

Renovating your town house's interior can be as easy as updating such cosmetic details as paint or wallpaper, or as extensive as gutting and reworking entire rooms. You can begin the process of transforming a floor of several small rooms into one large, radiant living room, great room, or master bedroom suite by knocking down interior walls and installing floor to ceiling windows. A simpler project might involve visually enlarging a small room by painting its walls a neutral shade such as magnolia or pale mushroom, since white or light colors visually recede. The room will feel even more spacious when you raise the ceiling visually with a white or pastel hue, and choose a pale, neutral carpet, or a light ceramic, bleached, or painted wood floor. Likewise, adding pale or neutral-hued upholstery and simple window treatments such as blinds, shades, or shutters will open up the space and maximize the light.

While some decorators scale down furnishings in small spaces, others recommend using a single oversize piece such as an armoire, bookcase, bed, or fireplace mantel to make a room's dimensions seem grander. Surprisingly, too many small furnishings will actually

OPPOSITE: *It's easy to create a sense of continuity between adjoining town house rooms by using the same wall color, flooring, and decorative style throughout. A welcoming sense of the past presides in this formal town house, where antique furnishings, heirloom china and silver, gilt mirrors, and architectural elements such as overdoors and cornice moldings create a picture of nineteenth-century elegance.*

emphasize a room's tiny area. A few other space-saving ideas include installing storage shelves that can be concealed behind movable panels; using built-in furniture wherever possible; and eliminating an extra staircase to add more square footage to a room. A town house located on a deep lot offers other creative possibilities: a several-story addition built on the rear of such a home will provide expanded living space and sumptuous garden views.

To welcome more light into dark foyers, some homeowners install skylights that shine down from the home's uppermost story. Other

ABOVE and OPPOSITE: *A graceful metal and wood staircase animates the neutral color scheme—a study in cream and tan—with its lively zigzagged profile and its striking modern design. The staircase ascends from the first-floor living room through several floors, past hallways featuring space-saving, built-in cupboards, until it reaches the top floor where it is crowned with a skylight, a radiant feature enjoyed by the home's owners and their sun-worshipping cat.*

popular window choices that add drama and light to any room include soaring Palladian windows, tasteful French doors, or tall sliding glass doors. For rooms without windows, some designers play up the intimate atmosphere to create cocoon-like libraries, media rooms, bedrooms, or even gallery-like dining rooms with "views" of landscape paintings. Warm palettes—bold reds, pumpkin, gold, rust, deep taupe—lend such rooms a cozy atmosphere. When windows are lacking, it's also a good idea to create a riveting focal point, such as an oversized painting hung above a fireplace.

In rooms graced with natural light, however, a cool palette of blue, green, or violet, or neutral white, gray, or beige furnishes a sense of calm serenity. And the illusion of added space and light can be created in any room with the clever use of mirrors. One mirrored wall alone will double the perceived size of a room. A tall, framed mirror can be positioned near a window in a living room or bedroom, for example, to reflect sunlight and the changing seasons. Also, a round, convex mirror will reflect an impressive global view of the room. Glass tables can likewise make a room feel larger, since these pieces tend to blur visual boundaries.

Maximizing space and light are also key considerations when updating an older town house's narrow, galley-style kitchen or renovating a tiny half bath, for example. Small kitchens will feel more expansive with the addition of one or more windows to bring in natural light. Keeping tall cabinetry and stacked appliances such as ovens and microwaves positioned at one end of the kitchen will open up counter space, which can serve as a work station, breakfast bar, or casual desk. Other small-space solutions include single sinks, which take up less space than double sinks, and light-reflecting metallic or light-colored countertops, appliances, and cabinetry, which add to a kitchen's clean, airy ambience. In old town house half baths, or "powder rooms," which are often situated near well-trafficked entry halls and living rooms, accentuating space and lighting when remodeling is as important as creating a sense of privacy and comfort. Such half baths generally include little more than a toilet, sink, mirror, and a few accessories. To improve this important guest room, you can install a window for warm, natural lighting and an outdoor view; angle a sink or install a sliding pocket door instead of a swinging door to free up floor space; cozy up the room with a striking palette such as lemon yellow, white, and sapphire blue or regal scarlet and gold; and add cheerful accessories such as fresh flowers, scented candles, plush towels, framed artwork or photos, and baskets of seashells or colorfully wrapped soaps.

Texture also plays a vital role in suggesting a feeling of space in rooms of minimal dimensions. By limiting busy patterns in your decor and choosing solid colored, richly textured wool or woven sisal carpets, grass cloth or suede-like wall coverings, and solid neutral or pastel brocaded upholstery,

for example, you can paint a monochromatic or light-hued scheme rich in visual accents. Also, highlighting such existing architectural details as classic moldings, door surrounds, and chair rails with crisp white paint can pay tribute to your town house's former life. By carrying the same cornices, door knobs, light switches, baseboards, and other design threads throughout every floor, you can weave a seamless tapestry of style that speaks eloquently of your home's harmonious character.

BELOW: *Designed with a welcoming, traditional decor, these town house social rooms are linked by gleaming parquet floors, richly appointed Victorian draperies and upholstery, and Adamesque doorways embellished with swags and fluted pilasters. The landscape mural in the music room serves as a focal point, enticing visitors from one room to the next.*

ABOVE: *Awash in color, texture, and pattern, this town house living room corner proves that compact spaces can easily become cherished places. This nook's sense of welcome and warmth radiates from its soft gold, antique matte walls, the window's olive green shutters and fresh flowers, and the comfy upholstered chairs and decorative pillows.*

OPPOSITE: *Along with mirrors, a tried and true visual trick that can make a room appear larger involves floor treatments. If you deliberately expose as much of your floor as possible by using wall-mounted tables and slender furnishings, the room appears more airy and spacious, as this elegant town house entryway proves.*

ABOVE: *A graceful window seat with serving table takes full advantage of this living room's bay window, making this the perfect spot for enjoying a cup of tea or relishing the garden view. Plump, richly textured pillows and the sparkling tea service embellished with fresh flowers adds to the room's delicious sophistication.*

OPPOSITE: *While the first floor of traditional upscale Victorian town houses typically featured an elaborate parlor, dining room, and sometimes a library, today you might find a luxurious living room or great room sited on the town house's top floor, especially if the view is captivating. Thinking "out of the box" about room placement, function, and design can help you transform your town house into a comfortable haven for your family and friends. This traditional town house living room, situated on an upper floor, artfully blends contemporary sofas with antique furnishings and accessories, presided over by ornate cornice moldings and lavishly appointed windows.*

OPPOSITE: *Spacious town house living rooms or family rooms that open onto libraries or music rooms, for example, can be easily subdivided with furniture to create cozy islands for conversation or quiet moments. In this traditional music room, an array of plush sofas, chairs, and a generous ottoman are arranged around a coffee table—the perfect spot for afternoon tea or reading. The living room that lies beyond the graceful columns also holds comfy places for relaxing or entertaining.*

ABOVE: *Linked to the music room by a warm yellow color scheme, ornate painted ceiling, lavish architectural columns and molding, and a grand antique rug, this living room offers an ambience of high-style welcome. Note how the delicate openwork loveseat and chairs and the combination of pink, cream, and yellow give this room a light, airy feel despite the grandiose, even overstated, architectural elements.*

ABOVE: *A terrace is a superb location for a garden room, which can effectively extend the family's living space and also extends the interior rooms visually. On the ground floor of this contemporary town house, an enclosed terrace enlarges the dining room and echoes the room's clean lines and minimalist feel.*

OPPOSITE: *In the same contemporary town house, a modern kitchen and casual dining area were designed to take advantage of such space-saving, built-in amenities as a kitchen island, wine racks, open and closed cupboards, bookshelves, and seating. Though the neutral color scheme is coolly modern, the warm tones of the wood and the sunny window down the hall give the room a sense of intimacy and cheer.*

BELOW: *Custom-built cabinets or bookcases, freestanding armoires, and cupboards not only provide key storage space in a compact town house—they can make a room appear larger by accentuating the room's horizontal or vertical lines. This relaxed town house family room offers a cozy built-in seat beneath an arched window, an entire wall of storage space for books, videos, and CDs, and contemporary furnishings accented with warm country touches.*

OPPOSITE: *During the 1850s, rising land costs prompted the building of narrow town houses in New York. While many town houses of the 1820s and 1830s had been designed to 30 feet (9m) in width, by midcentury they were 18- (5.5m) to 25- (7.5m) feet wide and extended from three to five stories high. This helps explain why the rooms of many vintage New York town houses seem compressed. Despite narrow dimensions, this formal town house dining room achieves a sense of spaciousness through its stunning wall murals, which add colorful, horizon-expanding views; stately, white pilasters accentuate the room's high ceilings, and open-back chairs lend an airy feel.*

ABOVE: *Skylights are a radiant feature of many late-nineteenth-century town houses as well as some contemporary examples. In older homes, skylights are often positioned above the main stairway so that sunlight can stream down from the top story to illuminate the entry hall. Skylights can also be found in upper-story master bedrooms and baths, kitchens, studios, libraries, and private nooks. This opulent corner hideaway is graced with Frank Lloyd Wright's barrel-style chairs, exquisitely crafted woodwork and flooring, elegant windows, and a luminous skylight.*

OPPOSITE: *This narrow galley-style town house kitchen was renovated with tall wooden cabinets, crisp white tiles and walls, and state-of-the-art appliances and lighting to create a fashionable, functional "heart of the home." The hanging pot-and-pan rack does double duty as a space-saving convenience and a stylish French country touch.*

RIGHT: *This sleek, minimalist living room creates an ambience of serenity with its creamy neutral furnishings, an artful mix of smooth and rough textures, a soaring ceiling, and an airy staircase, visible through the glass partition. The room's contrasting black and white color scheme provides an elegant setting for entertaining or private, pampered relaxation.*

ABOVE: *The welcome sense of light and space that mirrors can bring to any town house interior is dramatically evidenced in this contemporary bedroom. This immense mirror opens up an entire wall, visually expanding the size of the room. It has been thoughtfully placed across from a window in order to reflect the view outside whenever the drapes are open.*

ABOVE: *This town house bedroom with a view spotlights nature through its striking floor to ceiling windows, the room's focal point. Here, the designer has chosen a monochromatic color scheme, focusing on texture and pattern to create a light and lively effect. The animated upholstery pattern on the chair and the textured bedspread accent the scene, while the variegated glass bricks cast dappled shadows on the smooth floor.*

ABOVE: *Elegantly refined, this first-floor town house powder room exudes an ambience of tradition through its rich cinnamon-colored wallpaper and such key details as the antique mirror, brass towel holder, tasteful pedestal sink, framed artwork, and touches of nature. The shuttered window welcomes the sunlight in; slats close to provide privacy when desired.*

ABOVE: *The designer of this town house has created a luxurious master bath decked with floor-to-ceiling marble. The details— narrow windows, recessed lights, and glass-enclosed shower—combine to create an opulent, almost ethereal, retreat.*

CHAPTER FOUR
FORMAL DECORS

"It is delightful to transport one's self into the spirit of the past ..."

—Johann Wolfgang von Goethe

Public and private living spaces within the walls of restored or newly built Georgian- or Federal-style town houses are often charmingly formal, reminiscent of past times. From welcoming foyers to secluded master bedrooms, part of the allure of elegant period-style decor is its emphasis on architectural detail, from grand staircases to classical molding. For example, ceiling-level cornice moldings can add striking visual impact, framing an entire dining room or living room with a decorative band of swags and urns, Greek frets, or egg-and-dart motifs. For less elaborate rooms, cornice motifs such as simple concave, convex, or cove moldings add a classic, elegant touch. Chair rails, which are thin moldings applied thirty to forty inches (76 to 102cm) above the floor, protect the walls while offering visual appeal, as do a variety of baseboards, which range from a few inches to seven (18cm) or more inches in height.

Other architectural elements that provide historical detail and heighten an interior's visual drama include overdoors, which are architectural elements that perch above door frames; freestanding columns, which add monumental grandeur to doorways; decorative fireplace mantels; and of course, windows of all shapes and sizes, which connect the house's interior with its facade and the surrounding landscape.

A variety of formal, traditional interior design styles such as Federal, Victorian, and Art Deco are ideally suited for achieving period-style panache in town houses old and new. Federal decor was popular in the United States during the post-Revolutionary era of the late eighteenth and early nineteenth centuries. Among the hallmarks of Federal style interiors are elaborate architectural details such as Adamesque fireplace mantels and painted cornice moldings; expertly painted or finely detailed mahogany, cherry, walnut, rosewood, and bird's-eye maple furnishings; upholstery and festooned window treat-

OPPOSITE: *Every detail of this town house sitting room, from the lavish antique carpets and eclectic formal furnishings, to the heirloom collectibles and paintings, speaks of exquisite taste. The trompe l'oeil medallion motif on the arched ceiling provides a unifying design element that accentuates the room's length by drawing the eye to a dramatic vanishing point. During the Victorian era, plain or floral ceiling medallions of wood, plasterwork, or papier mâché were generally placed in the center of the ceiling, often encircling a decorative chandelier. Elaborately wallpapered ceilings also were popular throughout the Gilded Age.*

ments of chintz, brocade, silk, or toiles de Jouy; French scenic wallpapers; plaster walls painted Federal green, Williamsburg blue, mustard yellow, dark lavender, gray, or cream; chandeliers, candelabras, and romantic candles; and such accessories as blue and white Chinese porcelain, neoclassical urns and vases, and eagle motif mirrors—since the eagle was the symbol of the New Republic.

By today's standards, yesterday's formal Victorian interiors could easily be considered overdressed. To best appreciate their elaborate details, however, we need to recall that Victorian homes were designed to reflect good breeding, social standing, and wealth. Today's Victorian-inspired interiors can be as subtly or sumptuously ornate as desired, and may include such trademark touches as decorative plaster ceiling medallions, brackets, and cornices; lavishly trimmed sofas, ottomans, and easy chairs in plush or brocaded upholstery; refined cherry, oak, walnut, ash, and chestnut furnishings; polished wooden wainscoting, floors, staircases, and fireplace mantels; layered window treatments of velvet or damask for the winter, and cotton, chintz, muslin, or lace for the summer; richly patterned oriental rugs and flora and fauna wallpapers; such paint colors as bottle green, crimson, peacock blue, plum, olive, and terra-cotta; Victorian-style chandeliers, pendant lights, and wall sconces with art glass or frosted shades; and such decorative accessories as plants, needlework, knickknacks, gilt mirrors, bird cages, fringed shawls, and oil paintings.

Art Deco, an overwhelmingly popular design style of the late 1920s and 1930s, was influenced by several European design movements that emphasized bold, geometric motifs, vivid colors, and abstract floral forms. In North America, Art Deco was synonymous with the modern jazz era and Hollywood's Golden Age. Hallmarks of the luxurious Art Deco style include mirrored walls; open fireplaces with stepped profiles or facings of pastel tiles; exotic wooden furnishings and tubular, streamlined furnishings; wooden parquet floors and geometric-design linoleum floors; simple draperies with pelmets;

wallpapers sporting stylized leaves, flowers, fruit or chevrons; paint colors such as jade, purple, orange, cream, white, and muted greens, blues, yellows, and pinks; fan-shaped uplights and floor lights, and chandeliers with geometric motifs; and such accessories as zebra and leopard skins, and Art Deco–style figurines, cigarette trays, clocks, and vases.

Whether you choose a period-perfect, traditional decorating scheme or an eclectic blending of formal contemporary furnishings with a few Federal-, Victorian-, or Art Deco–style pieces and accessories, you're sure to achieve your goal—a town house interior that echoes another era with unforgettable welcome and warmth.

OPPOSITE: *During the Victorian era, a variety of decorating motifs—Gothic, neo-Rococo, neo-Renaissance, Moorish, Scottish Baronial—enjoyed periods of popularity. These styles often mingled with one another in the lavish, eclectic, Gilded-Age home. In this period-perfect Victorian town house library, a world of design influences are evident. From the Adamesque mantel to the exotic oriental rug and kilim chair cushion, the Victorian aesthetic welcomes the happy coexistence of even the most diverse styles.*

ABOVE: *This inviting Federal-style living room bears such decorative touches as the ornate fireplace mantel and molded panels flanking the windows. More elaborate design motifs— festoons, husks, urns, scrolling foliage, cornucopias—often appear over windows and in fireplace surrounds of Federal-style town house decors. The color scheme in cream, gold, and scarlet completes the charming period look.*

OPPOSITE: *Generous built-in bookcases line the hallway leading to an eclectic town house living room. A frieze with a Greek key pattern and the hall's near-perfect symmetry—note the lamps and framed medallions—echo the formality of the living room, where pieces are arranged with precision on either side of a columned fireplace. The space is gracious yet lively, thanks to unlikely combinations such as marble busts set beside claw-footed chairs upholstered in vivid crimson with black trim.*

ABOVE: *Layers of texture, pattern, and color are artfully combined in this small but still stately room. By mixing patterns that share a similar palette, in this case deep reds and olives with accents of black, and including some restful solids, this home decorator has avoided a too-busy feeling. A stenciled frieze, echoed on curtain edges, and gilt framed etchings and mirror decorate the wall space; because the pieces are relatively large and balance one another well, the wall looks full but not cluttered.*

OPPOSITE: *Popular after the War of Independence, America's Federal style of interior design was influenced by British cabinetmaker George Hepplewhite's furnishings, British and French studies of antiquity, and British architect Robert Adam's delicate neoclassical designs. In this formal Federal-style dining room, an elegantly swagged bay window, decorative fireplace, ornate architectural embellishments, and fine furnishings and accessories speak of late eighteenth- and early nineteenth-century elegance.*

RIGHT: *These adjoining town house rooms display exuberant Gilded-Age eclecticism, where Federal and neoclassical style meet and mingle with the Victorian style's fascination with the Orient. Here, reproduction Federal-style furnishings upholstered in rich, regal fabrics are boldly juxtaposed with a mix of intricately patterned rugs for an animated effect. The Greek vase prints and the sculpted bust perched on a pedestal speak of an abiding love for the past.*

OPPOSITE: *A chef's dream, this Victorian-inspired kitchen has a vintage pressed-tin ceiling and beadboard wainscoting. The wallpaper frieze sports a floral Arts and Crafts motif, and the island and glass front storage cabinet are made of sturdy oak, a Victorian favorite. But the real focal point of this kitchen is the wall of cast iron and polished copper cookware. The immense pot rack not only creates a stunning display, it's also a clever space-saving device.*

RIGHT: *Some designers accentuate the slender confines of Victorian town house parlors and dining rooms to create rooms that look and feel like opulent nineteenth-century railroad cars. Here the rich table setting and jewel-toned walls, curtains, and chairs evoke an elegant cloister.*

LEFT: *Ralph Waldo Emerson once said, "Things are pretty, graceful, rich, elegant, handsome, but until they speak to the imagination, not yet beautiful." The breathtaking shell of this Victorian bedroom enchants with its ornate ceiling and ceiling medallion, its decorative frieze, and its softly muted colors. The room's stylish but understated furnishings set off, rather than compete with, the room's impressive architectural elements.*

RIGHT: *During the nineteenth century, Queen Victoria's daughter, Princess Vicky, built a small country palace that featured lovely, simply appointed rooms bedecked with her favorite collectibles. When it came to decorating, she espoused a simple philosophy: "Everything to please, nothing to impress." Today, many designers agree that our homes should be personal sanctuaries rather than showplaces. This understated town house bedroom enchants with its ornate, Victorian fan-style window, lovely antique bed and mirror, and a few beloved accessories—a pleasant retreat free of excessive ornamentation.*

ABOVE: *The spirit of Victorian elegance reigns in this unforgettable town house bathroom. The stunning nature-inspired stained-glass windows and marble tile walls are doubled by the mirrored wall alongside the bathtub, which enlarges the space, increases the light, and multiplies the decorative effect. A palette of jade green and rich gold heightens the opulent ambience.*

LEFT: *This high-Victorian bathroom is not only a private retreat for grooming and bathing but a gallery of sorts for beloved prints, paintings, and collectibles. Here, the artwork and figurines speak to the Victorian love of the exotic. Designed to reflect good breeding, social standing, and wealth, the well-dressed Victorian bathroom was lavishly decorated with chandeliers, knickknacks, framed paintings, richly upholstered furniture, and even elaborate-stained glass windows.*

CHAPTER FIVE

CONTEMPORARY & CASUAL INTERIORS

"Beauty of style and harmony and grace and good rhythm depend on simplicity."

—*PLATO*

While many town house facades speak eloquently of architectural tradition, their interiors often showcase the unexpected. Instead of formal, traditional decor, many vintage and contemporary town houses reflect their owners' eclectic tastes and penchant for clean modern, eclectic, or country-inspired interiors perfect for both everyday living and sophisticated entertaining.

While formal rooms enchant with their dressy arrangements of prized antique or reproduction furnishings, lavish window treatments, and period accessories, relaxed, pared-down settings can be just as appealing and memorable. To plan such a simplified, personalized decor, it's important for you to consider what makes your living spaces comfortable and functional. Whether you're planning to redecorate your town house's living room, kitchen, great room, or a bedroom, you'll want to choose furnishings, accessories, and wall, window, and floor treatments that appeal to your sense of sight and touch. Rooms that feature stereo sound systems, melodic wind chimes, or tabletop fountains can also delight with lovely orchestrated or natural music. Bouquets of flowers and scented candles heighten a room's serene, sensual ambience, as can healing, natural sunlight welcomed in through sheer lace panels, pleated shades, simple valances, or shutters.

Color is also an important consideration when creating a comfortable living space. Quiet, neutral colors such as bisque, gray, caramel, or beige, or soft pastels including pink, peach, blue, or green, paint a gentle background that's easy on the eyes. Such hues can be energized by myriad textures, including wicker, straw, wood, stone, velvet, suede, nubby wool, leather, and smooth glass. A few key patterns in floral, striped, or checked upholstery, or in Southwestern throws or rustic camp blankets, can add personality to any easygoing decor.

Numerous interior design styles are ideally suited for creating an ambience of relaxed elegance within the town house. You can create a casual look with a sleek modern, colorful eclectic, or charming country-style approach.

The clutter-free appeal of modern decor can be achieved with clean-lined furnishings that work especially well with the vertically oriented spaces of modern town houses. In the narrow rooms of older

OPPOSITE: *This narrow living room achieves a sense of contemporary elegance and spaciousness through its high ceiling and airy design, an emphasis on subtle neutral colors and natural woods, a variety of smooth and rough textures, clean-lined modern furnishings in complementary colors, and an open staircase spotlighted by recessed and hanging lights.*

town houses, low slung, midcentury modern furnishings and contemporary modular pieces present a dramatic juxtaposition with traditional architecture. Other striking features of modern town house decor include warm textured upholstery in natural silks, leathers, suedes, wools, and weaves; neutral or pastel-colored walls; bold ethnic fabrics and rugs; smooth marble, glass, metal, and lacquered furnishings; tile, stone, brick, and parquet floors; simple blinds and Roman shades or shutters; recessed and track lighting and contemporary uplights; and a chosen few vivid paintings and accessories. To achieve a more minimalist aesthetic, you can pare down a modern decor to a few understated furnishings, undress your windows and floors, and spotlight such simple accessories as shimmering metal candlesticks, framed black and white photos, or glass vases filled with statuesque lilies or soft pussy willows. Such thoughtful editing draws attention to a room's architectural details, its unfettered natural lighting, gleaming wooden or stone floors, clean neutral palette, and its sense of openness and serenity.

An eclectic approach to room design offers you the freedom to mix tasteful furnishings and accessories of different eras that share a common theme such as color, pattern, or perhaps a formal or relaxed character. When the room's key colors are deliberately repeated in furnishings or accessories, you achieve a sense of balance and harmony—creating an artful, unique setting for your old and new treasures. An informal mood is assured with the infusion of rough-textured surfaces, such as coir carpets or scrubbed pine tables, and personable country-style bouquets or baskets of seashells.

American or European country-style decors can also offer lighthearted charm to any of your favorite town house retreats, from kitchens to family rooms, bedrooms to baths. Such unpretentious decors introduce a sense of the past and a reverence for nature, showcasing wooden beams and rustic plank floors, carved and painted wooden furnishings and folk art, rugged stone walls and fireplaces,

OPPOSITE and ABOVE: *The decor of a town house interior is limited only by one's imagination. This New York town house has been designed to achieve a lodgelike ambience. The entry hall celebrates the great outdoors with its thriving plant life and rugged stone wall. The same stonework reappears in the living room, where the cozy atmosphere is maintained by overstuffed chairs, Navajo rugs, and an inviting fireplace. Complete with Arts and Crafts–style tables, bookshelves, and light fixtures, the home manages to be both rustic and urbane.*

slate, limestone, and brick floors, lovely flora-and-fauna-patterned wallpaper and upholstery, an array of antiques and collectibles, fresh flowers and plants, and much, much more. From rustic American country style with its muted milk paint hues to the flower-bedecked English cottage style and the vibrant French-country interiors, peaceful country-style rooms beckon with comfort, color, and coziness, as well as with the romance of the great outdoors and furnishings and accessories made from nature's gifts.

No matter what spirited interior design style you choose to reflect your passions and indulge your senses, a relaxed approach is sure to imbue your favorite town house retreats with unforgettable personality and comfort.

R I G H T : *Space-expanding elements can be cleverly employed to enlarge a room's dimensions. In this relaxed yet proper town house living room, two islands of angled furniture groupings make the living space appear wider, while cream-colored architectural elements such as ceiling moldings and door and window surrounds make the ceiling appear higher. The rich palette of gold, cream, taupe, and brown imbues the room with warmth and creates a greater sense of space and light.*

LEFT: *A striking corridor of light, this narrow town house dining room offers an exquisite place to soak up the sunshine while reading the morning paper. The stunning skylight not only bathes the room in light, it also makes the dimensions seem grander. Generous French doors open onto a terrace that harbors a lush garden room, extending the dining area out of doors.*

OPPOSITE: *If each room in a town house is a painter's canvas, then this room is a folk art masterpiece. Adorned with carefully chosen antique furnishings—a carved antique bedstead decked with handmade quilts and pillows made with vintage textiles—this charming bedroom has true American country spirit. The rustic barn board floor ties all the elements together and the unadorned windows let in plenty of warmth and light, completing the homey look.*

ABOVE: *Classic ebony and gold elements are dramatically juxtaposed with contemporary art, furniture, and ceramics in this sleek town house dining room. The room's focal point—the town house's spectacular terrace—is the perfect setting for after-dinner entertaining.*

ABOVE: *Color can work magic in a room blessed with abundant architectural details. Notice how the light-hued architectural elements—from the built-in cabinetry to the recessed, shuttered windows—stand out from the darker, chocolate-colored walls in this spirited dining room. The somewhat formal furnishings and table setting are cheerfully lightened by an eclectic assortment of sculpted art, from the wooden hands on the cabinet to the black iron wall ornaments.*

LEFT: *This streamlined, contemporary town house kitchen earns rave reviews for style and efficiency. Intersecting planes unite kitchen, dining room, and second floor into a single geometric composition. Sleek, state-of-the-art appliances become additional geometric elements, perfectly complementing the decor and making this kitchen as beautiful as it is functional.*

OPPOSITE: *A closer view of the town house dining room reveals the room's spaciousness and architectural details, typical highlights of minimalist decor. Here, intersecting planes in a wide variety of materials and textures—brushed stainless steel, polished concrete, gleaming blond wood, frosted translucent glass—create a lively, though neutral-colored, ambience. Clean-lined furnishings and a few decorative touches, in the form of the blue suede dining room chairs and curvilinear fruit tray, are all that's needed to accent the sleek look.*

OPPOSITE: *Storage space abounds in this minimalist town house bedroom, where built-in closets and dressers contribute to carefree living. A stark, clean palette of black, white, and gray adds a feeling of airiness to the room—a crisp sanctuary designed for peaceful relaxation far from the frenetic pace of city life.*

ABOVE: *In North America and around the world, blue and white palettes have long been popular for home interiors. To many people, blue represents infinity, serenity, spirituality, or trustworthiness. When combined with white, cream, or ivory, blue can speak boldly or softly, and its personality can be cool and tranquil or positively sunny, depending upon the warm or cool accent colors used in the room. The designers of this town house retreat cleverly added a touch of warmth to the bedroom with yellow pillows, a lemon-hued table lamp, and an oil painting in a golden oak frame.*

OPPOSITE: *Alluring eclectic rooms are never just "thrown together." They're the result of a carefully planned marriage of furnishings and accessories that may vary in style but share similar colors, textures, or patterns. This eclectic town house bathroom sparkles with a lovely Victorian clawfoot tub, pedestal sink, and tile floor that complement perfectly modern textured tiles and a charming window pane wall cabinet.*

RIGHT: *Like many of today's renovated town houses, this home's state-of-the-art kitchen offers both convenience and style. The kitchen is typically narrow, yet long, so there is adequate room for cupboards, appliances, and working counter space. The owners of this house added more light and drama to the kitchen by installing several tall, colorful, Frank Lloyd Wright–inspired windows, truly the room's dramatic focal point.*